In Pursuit of
the Almost

In Pursuit of the Almost

Published by Endeavor Literary Press
P.O. Box 49272
Colorado Springs, Colorado 80949

www.endeavorliterary.com

ISBN Hardback: 978-1-7368734-0-3
ISBN Paperback: 978-1-7368734-1-0

Cover Design: James Clarke, United Kingdom (jclarke.net)

In Pursuit of
the Almost

PHIL GINSBURG

ENDEAVOR
LITERARY PRESS

Contents

Dedication

Anywhere but here with you is elsewhere and elsewhere is ultimately nowhere without you.

"Normality is a paved road: It's comfortable to walk, but no flowers grow on it."

Vincent van Gogh

Truth Be Told

"I saw truth flick a cigarette at those guys."

"Truth don't even smoke," somebody else said.

Another witness remarked, "Truth didn't do anything;
the guys in the car shot for no reason."

Three people said truth started saying stuff,
stuff nobody wanted to hear.
Some people told truth to shut up,
but truth kept jawing at everybody.

An elderly woman said truth was in the wrong neighborhood,
had no reason to be there, especially at that hour.

Somebody said truth needed to get its head on straight,
needed some correction.
One woman, who refused to reveal her identity,
said the witnesses were liars.

Everybody was coming from a different angle.
Every cusp of a cause was claiming their truth was real truth.

Someone discovered truth had been shot in the back.
Apparently, truth tried to walk away from the scene that night—
wasn't looking for a fight.

Someone suggested that truth was a victim of mistaken identity.
Perhaps the guys in the car thought truth
was truth's half-brother—
half-truth.
That happens a lot.

Five suspects, alleged to have been in the car that night,
were brought in for questioning.
Nobody admitted to anything.

No one at the crime scene
would go to the lineup to identify anyone.
You couldn't blame them.
If they would kill truth,
they wouldn't hesitate to kill friends of the truth.

You should have seen truth's funeral.
People from every race,
neighborhood,
income,
political affiliation,
religion,
showed up.

Who knew truth had touched so many lives?

Many testified that truth tried to make a difference.
Wasn't afraid of being unpopular.
Repaired their marriages.
Enabled them to face conflicts and overcome addictions.

One man even claimed
that truth helped him
give up
fried calamari.
It was very moving.

At the cemetery, as they lowered the coffin into the ground,
(You may not believe this, but I was there and saw it happen),
truth opened the casket and got out,
looked at everyone, and said,
"I'm not dead. You can't kill me. I'm still here."

Then truth walked off the cemetery grounds—
in grave clothes—
crossed the street,
went into a Chinese takeout place and,
five minutes later,
got on a bus
with a carton of chicken-fried rice.

Some people were upset.
"Where did truth get money for bus fare and food?"

Others blamed the media for hyping truth's death,
(no doubt to further their agendas).

Reportedly, truth was seen the following week,
at a police interrogation in Damascus,
a divorce court in Akron,
a perjury hearing in Allentown, Pennsylvania,
a confessional booth in Holland,
and at a high school audition for *Cats* in Branson, Missouri.

Truth, I found out, was recently stabbed
in a domestic dispute
in Richmond, Virginia,
but survived.

Truth, it seems, gets around a lot.
But maybe not as much as some folks
get around the truth.

Them

They are taking the poetry out of life.
They are robbing us of the words
that create the images,
that fertilize the orchard of the heart,
where the daring diversity of thought can still grow.

Now the noises of novices,
with fragmented sentences of addiction to power,
seek to silence us into submission,
to the sad certitude of their whipped cream convictions.

Over my dead body.

Already decomposing
another thought into words,
words that will pull the pin
and leave shrapnel of truth
in the thin-skinned flayers
of freedom.

But Who's Counting?

Sheltered in place for sixty-eight days,
but who's counting?

Without a haircut for eighty-two days,
but who's counting?

Gained four pounds in six days,
but who's counting?

Haven't seen my daughter in 107 days,
but who's counting?

Zoomed a friend nine days ago,
but who's counting?

Down to last the eight blood pressure meds,
but who's counting?

Lost job 126 days ago,
but who's counting?

Rent due in five days,
but who's counting?

Three cans of black beans,
half pound of rice,
a pound of freezer-burned chopped meat,
and two kids to feed,
but who's counting?

Friend in ICU for thirteen days,
but who's counting?

Ten days with no call from boss about
getting my job back,
but who's counting?

Twenty-five days 'til summer,
but who's counting?

And you wonder every day,
when will this end?
Will you ever be the same?
Does your life even matter?

And is there still time
to do that one thing
on earth
we were placed here to do?

And is there someone
who still believes in you,
someone who will never stop believing in you,
that someone who's still counting
that your life really counts?

If you don't have someone like that in your life,
I pray that one day you will,
especially now.

And if you remember,
please pray I will too.

Meanwhile, it's all good.
According to my Facebook page,
I have 818 friends.

But who's counting?

Plagues of Possibility

Blueberries fell from the sky that April Tuesday morning,
all over the world, "like a plague," people said.

From Moscow to Memphis:
cars damaged,
roofs ruined,
pavements pockmarked with blue rage.
Rivers of blueberry juice submerged cities.
Stock markets all over the world went kaput.
People in Denmark went compote.

Farmers in Maine, the Blueberry State, were particularly upset.
"What's the point of growing this stuff if people can get it for
free?"

In Helsinki, they made blueberry vodka.
In Panama, pies.
In Malta, muffins.

"It's a sign from God," people said.

"Why would God send blueberries down on us?"

The world questioned.

The blueberries stayed fresh for five days.
Then they started to rot and stink.
Soon rats and vermin caused a piggyback plague.
No pigs were involved.

"We are cursed," people said.

However, millions of people were hired
as Cyanococcus cleanup crews.
Skills were birthed.
The economy improved.

"God has blessed our land," others said.

Street corner prophets preached of a huckleberry
hell that awaits the unrepentant.
Fats Domino, at eighty-five, enjoyed a career revival.
He appeared on the David Letterman Show
singing "Blueberry Hill."

Jerry Metz was on his way that Tuesday morning
to meet that woman,
that woman who was not his wife.
He was asking for a sign if it was right.

Then the blueberries fell and he knew (he just knew)
that the plague was sent for him.
He took it that way.
Jerry took everything that way.
Personally.

After that day, blueberries never fell from the sky again.
People went back to their routines.
For blueberry growers, pickers, and supermarkets,
it was business as usual.
The cleanup crews received unemployment benefits.
They secretly hoped another plague of possibility
would happen again soon.

And it did.

A month after the blueberry plague,
Jerry drove on a Tuesday morning to meet
that woman
again.

This time mounds of lemon zest
fell from the sky.
Jerry again took it as a sign.
Drove straight to work.
Decided he would never,
ever see that woman

again.

"I'm going to avoid her like the plague," he said.

Jerry, it seems, was spiritually sensitive.

In June of the same year,
on yet another Tuesday morning,
latex-free band-aids fell all over the world,
at the moment Juanita Mendez in the Bronx
went after her husband Carlos with a serrated steak knife
because he had violated another restraining order.

Looking up at the sky,
Juanita dropped the knife.
She and Carlos held one another
as thousands of winged adhesives
glided across Alexander Avenue
as gently as a great grey owl in flight.

"God knows we all need healing," she sighed.

I think she spoke for everyone that morning,
from Moscow to Memphis.

God knows we all need healing.

The Things I've Heard

I've heard of deaf people who suddenly hear,
and hearing people who gradually go deaf.

I've heard of pedicures that lasted longer than three hours,
and people with six toenails.

I've heard of people who wanted to live and died,
and people who wanted to die, jumped off buildings, took pills,
and lived.

I've heard of famous people being unhappy,
and obscure people wanting to be famous.

I heard that you loved me,
but didn't think I loved you.

I've heard of people talking about the end of the world,
and couples planning to have more children.

I have heard of people returning from near-death experiences,
and others searching for near-life experiences.

Oh, the things I've heard.

I've heard of kind letters never sent,
and hurtful letters arriving right on time.

I've heard things spoken behind my back,
and things I've told myself in the mirror.

I've heard your median income is $76,700,
and that you don't feel anyone values you.

I have heard of nations planning war,
and how peace is not hard to find when you know where to look.

I've heard of relationships going sour,
and people staying sweet even when they've been offended.

I've heard of boxing matches being fixed,
and that an overcooked duck can never be fixed.

I have heard of politicians who never keep promises,
and people who keep vows even when it hurts.

I have heard of comedians who are depressed,
and depressed people who wish they could do standup comedy.

I've heard that your medication doesn't work anymore,
and that your doctor secretly thinks only a miracle will heal you.

I've heard of prayers that were answered,
and prayers that never had a prayer of being answered.

All these things I've heard
and thousands more.
I heard that you loved me,
but didn't think I loved you.

I'm sorry.

I've never been a good listener.

Another Tale of Two Cities

I was in my apartment on West 46th Street years back when I heard a commotion on the street. I looked out my window and two guys, with car doors open, were ready to square off in the middle of 9th Avenue traffic.

"Blessed are the peacemakers for they shall be called the children of God."

I decided I had to do something and went downstairs to the street and approached the two.

"What happened?" I asked.

They both started screaming again.

"Why don't you both drive around the corner, park, and talk it over?" I suggested. "You're going to get killed standing here."

"He'll drive away!" one remarked.

"Okay," I said, "I'll go with him. If he drives away, he has to take me too."

I noticed both cars had Jersey plates. I was born in Jersey. I didn't want to spend another night there. I got in the car and we drove around the corner and parked with the other driver right behind us. I thought, *What am I gonna do now?*

Immediately a patrol car turned the corner. I waved at them to stop as if I had just witnessed a murder.

I proceeded to go back upstairs to my apartment, where I was fully expecting a call from the Nobel people in Sweden.

Today, I'm on a bagel hunt in downtown Colorado Springs.

It's 9:30 in the morning and I notice two guys on the corner are ready to square off. A young white guy is doing a bad impression of Joe Frazier—hands up, weaving and bobbing. His adversary is a short Mexican man in his fifties who just stands there. What bothers me is the white guy's girlfriend. She doesn't intervene.

I think she wants her boyfriend to turn the Mexican guy's face into salsa. I don't get in the middle of this one. I say a silent prayer and walk into the bagel shop.

When I come out, the Mexican guy is sitting on a park bench, his face intact. All is quiet and nobody is hurt.

I have a feeling that scenes like this are being played out in cities all over our country now—frustrated young white guys wanting to punch out small foreign-looking guys while their girlfriends look on.

I buy a half-dozen bagels and eat two hot sesame seed ones before I get to my car, and then I eat a poppy seed bagel while driving home.

NORAD, the air defense system for the nation, is here. Every day I am conscious that this is the day we'll be nuked. I don't want to die with a half-dozen hot bagels on the front seat of my car.

At home, my wife asks, "What happened to the other bagels?"

I shrug and say, "NORAD."

She's heard all this before.

"If you die, you go to heaven and the bagels won't matter," she says.

I'm only half listening. I'm troubled by why the white guy's girlfriend was so bloodthirsty and why I didn't cross the street and extend the combatants an olive branch, or at least a blueberry bagel.

I'm eating a fourth bagel now: cinnamon raisin.

"There's only two raisins in the entire bagel!" I yell in the kitchen. "We're standing at Ground Zero for God's sake. Put some raisins in these bagels!"

It's now the third month since I lost my job, and it's a far, far cry from 9th Avenue, where I once made peace in the middle of traffic between two jerks from Jersey.

I'm still waiting for a call from Sweden.

Body Language

I asked my eyes this morning: "What happened?
You once looked at the world with so much love."

My eyes said: "We don't know. We haven't changed.
Maybe you changed."

"Will I ever see the world the same way again?" I asked.

"Remains to be seen," they said.

At least my eyes haven't lost their sense of humor.

My ears don't hear the sound of love like they once did, either.

"What happened?" I asked.

"Hey, we haven't changed," they said.
"We still hear, but you stopped listening."

That hurt.

My feet commented that I had been stepping
on people's feelings for a while,
that I had gone backward in my growth as a person.

That hurt.

My brain said it remembered
when I thought about love all the time.
It missed the feel-good chemicals.

"It's the thought that counts," brain said.

"You sound like a greeting card," I told it.

"Anything would be improvement on you," brain replied.

Brains hold grudges.

My hands said I was too busy
grasping for things of little value.
I didn't argue.

My nose said it lost its ability
to discern the fragrance of
people's feelings.

"Well, it's allergy season," I replied. "You're stuffed up."

"Don't blame nature," nose sniffed.

My lungs, once oxygenated with gratitude,
complained that my shallowness
caused shortness of breath.

My thyroid remained silent,
but its look spoke volumes.

My voice said I once spoke of love all the time.
It had no words for what happened to me.
What could I say?

Finally, I asked my heart,
"What happened to my ability to love?"

"I go to bed every night asking the same question,"
my heart replied. "I don't know, but I can help.
First apologize to your body parts
for the distress you've caused. We're all in this together."

"Thanks," I said. "I will."

And I did.

It took two weeks for the body parts to forgive me.
Brain was the last to respond.
It refused to let go of its grudges
until I handed it a two-scoop cone of chocolate
custard dipped in sprinkles.

It cost me five dollars.
But brain was right.

It is the thought that counts,
at least chemically speaking.

Five dollars for an ice cream cone.
Love always comes with a cost.

Rush Hour

I will probably never die a Midwest death,
like in a grain elevator accident.

That's a relief.

I would prefer to spend my last
mortal moments on the East Coast
clutching my chest
on the West 96th Street subway platform,
falling in front of the oncoming
number two express train during rush hour.

The passengers on the two train will, of course,
have to switch tracks and take the one train
(due to my inconvenient death).

The last words I imagine hearing
are those of Luis Cruz.

He's saying to his pregnant girlfriend, Wanda,
"Why couldn't that selfish
piece of shit have died
in a grain elevator accident
on some farm in Kansas?"

I think I hear Wanda reply,
"I'm really in the mood for pistachio ice cream."

I remember, a second before,
seeing the face of God
while wishing
I had met Wanda
forty years earlier
under different circumstances.

Without, of course, Luis.

Hope With Toppings

I've gained weight.
My doctor asked if my diet had changed.
I told him I had been gorging on hope.
He said, "You need to monitor that, because hope
deferred will make your heart sick."

Turns out he was right.
The next day Hope decided I needed,
for a season,
a diet of disappointment.

"It would be good for you," he said.
"You'll thank me for it later."

Sure enough,
overnight,
the promises I once fed on
began to taste like hospice haute cuisine—
like pimento cream cheese tea sandwiches
served as afternoon snacks to the terminally ill.

My heart went on a hunger strike.
They force-fed me an intravenous solution of positive
placebos and eventually released me.

But something happened last night
amid the movable feast of the unforeseeable.
Hope showed up at my door
with a three-topping, sixteen-inch pizza.

Turns out he had the wrong address.
It was for Lucille,
my next-door neighbor,
who recently lost her husband, Mike,
to pancreatic cancer.

I was happy the pizza was for her.
She, too, had suffered a diet of disappointment
for a season.

Five minutes later
she called and asked
if I would help her eat that pie.
Of course, I said yes.

We ate.
We talked.
We laughed.
I liked the pineapple topping.

With every bite,
we felt an appetite
for hope rising within us,
like one of those self-rising pizza crusts
they advertise on television.

Speaking of crusts,
Lucille said the crust on our pizza
tasted nothing like those awful
hospice haute cuisine tea sandwiches.

And I had every reason to believe her.

Key Issues

My keys are missing.
They ran away from home.
Tired of locks. And slots. Tired of turning.
Right. Left. Left. Right.

Tired of entrances and exits.
Tired of ignition penetrations.
Tired of pockets with used tissues and crumpled cash.

Tired of clicks and clangs
on the same ring of repetition.
Tired of doing the daily dance
alongside the plastic supermarket
and library ID tags.

Tired of jagged edge existence.
They got bored.
Time to move on, they reasoned.
There has to be more to life than this.

I feel badly for them.
Even if found by strangers,
they won't fit anywhere.
They will discover,
as all runaway keys do,
that it's a jangle out there.

They will seek to find their way back home.
Too late, I fear.
Like the title of Thomas Wolfe's novel,
You Can't Go Home Again.

Wolfe was right.
They will be replaced with identical slot seekers,
dead ringers of the previous danglers,
dancing next to the same ID shimmy shakers.

Perhaps the new notches
will one day feel too big for their niches.
They too will choose to go out on their own.
Leave home.
Look for new ways to find their groove.
Unlock their potential.

Without ever reading a single page of Wolfe's novel.

Thoughts While Having a Heart Attack

Death came the other day and tried to take my breath away.

How do you bid breath to stay and not take its leave,
when breath no longer has strength to breathe?

Poised in pain to now imprint the floor,
I spot the raspberry Jell-O I spilled ten minutes before.

My gurney journey, now in full throttle.
The hallway, now a blur of every IV bottle.

Will my whole life now pass before my eyes?
Or will it be the life of Cary Grant or Karl Marx
or some other surprise?

Death now enters the surgical room dressed in gray.
I've seen better suits on Goodwill senior discount day.
I suppose, maybe, Death only wears dead men's clothes.

"Your last breath is now mine to take away," says he.

"Oh Death," I reply,
"are you so dead that you never heard what my Master said?"
'He who believes in me shall never die.'"

So death left with no goodbye.
I'm sure he'll return one day,
hopefully with a different tie.

What else could I tell him? What else could I say?
For love
stronger than death
has already claimed my every breath.

God's love
every day
takes my breath
away.

Despite needing my CPAP machine
to breathe at night.

You Never Know

You never know when it will come.
You can't track it like a FedEx package.
That moment,
when all the other moments
leading up to that moment,
whisper, "I told you."

That call, that apology,
that idea long buried
and now resurrected.

That look, that smile,
that gesture, that prayer,
that friend, that recipe.

That moment
when the bread
you once cast on the water
comes back covered
with butter and grape jelly.

You never know when
those with the means
will bring things to an end.

You never know when
the propane tank will leak
and leave you
with third-degree brisket burns.

You never know if
you'll make it through
the fourth inning,
the third quarter,
the tenth round.

You never know if
you'll find the one thing
that makes all the other things
one.

You never know if
it was your fault,
their fault,
nobody's fault.

You never know if
the pizza guy at your door
lost his faith in God
on the way to your house.

You never know what
was behind her words,
his silence.

You never know until
they retrieve the little black box
in the field,
amid open luggage,
exposed undergarments,
and a one-way ticket to Montreal.

Then you know
what was behind her words,
his silence,
and that it was
never your fault.

Yen King

One summer in the city, I wanted to end it all.
I was so depressed I didn't have the energy to kill myself.
The only thing that kept me alive was the Chinese
restaurant being built across the street from my hotel.

I decided I would go on opening day.
It would be my last meal, like a prisoner's, on death row.

I waited three months for the place to be built.
And then came the big day,
when they put out red, white, and blue flags.

I dressed in a sports jacket.

I wasn't ready to eat in public, so I ordered takeout.
I brought an egg-drop soup,
fried rice,
and noodle dish
back to my room.
The plan was to eat and die.
I wasn't going to open the fortune cookie.

The food was awful: salty, greasy.
The soup carton leaked.
I had prolonged my useless life for three months
for this moment?

I started to laugh,
the first laugh in a year.

Then I laughed more, and more, and soon
I was laughing so hard.
I was crying and laughing.
There was fried rice and noodles all over me.
I didn't care.

That day
I decided that
life was better than death.

And then I opened the fortune cookie.

To Somebody Out Here

When you're at the end of your rope,
on the scaffold of hope,
no matter what,
get loose from the noose,
and say no to the knot,
"I've got better things to do
than hanging out with you."

Dorothy Parker Discovers
Someone Unfollowed Her

I will unfollow you wherever you go.
Your every post is now just toast.
I no longer need to know
what you have for breakfast
when you leave for Tokyo.

You unfollowed me in 2019,
sometime in the fall.
Was it something I said that caused
your conscience to careen off my wall?

What's left to do,
but to unfollow you.

No more to like or share
on what we do, with whom, and where.
It's kind of comforting to know
that neither of us no longer care.

At first it was a bit hard to swallow
that you decided first to unfollow.
You must have thought my life
perhaps a shade hollow.

No argument from me.
I would probably agree.

Perhaps, in the end,
to unfollow one another is not a waste,
but an affirmation
that should not leave
our hearts bereft.

For from this mutual displeasure,
we discover that what is left is nothing less
than a confirmation of the good taste
we both instinctively possess.

Remembering Eddie

Found out a friend from high school died last week.
Eddie Goldberg.

In the tenth grade, Eddie, Larry Katz, and I
sang on stage in our high school auditorium
in front of three hundred kids and faculty.

"Them bones,
them bones gonna rise again,
now hear the word of the Lord."

Three Jewish kids
singing an old gospel song
about Israel's rising from spiritual osteoporosis
and returning to faith.

The audience threw pennies at us—
we counted twenty-seven cents.

I wonder if my biology teacher Mr. Paul contributed.
He always had a habit of adding his two cents.

I hope my dead bones,
with Eddie's and Larry's,
will rise together on that
Great Resurrection day.

Maybe we will sing that same song,
together in the New Jerusalem
as angels toss loose change at us
while Ella Fitzgerald sings "Pennies from Heaven."

It will be a glorious memory of that morning on stage.
The first time I got paid for singing in public.

And the last.

St. Carol at Walmart

This morning I am in need of a heavenly language,
to speak in the tongues of angels,
because I am in the presence of one,
in Walmart, of all places,
specifically, the pharmacy.

Carol bags my ninety-day supply of a beta blocker.
It will keep the heart rhythms from mimicking
a heavy metal drummer.

Who is Carol really?

Her countenance appears to be scripted
with a divine dosage of kindness.
Her eyes, canonized in compassion,
offer refills of tenderness
to those of us in need of a supplement of humanity
along with our Ambien and Zoloft.

I watch as she staples the bag of insulin for Harry
and offers him a glance
so warm
it melts his heart like—
that now forbidden—
dark chocolate hazelnut truffle
he once buried in the glove compartment
of a July memory

while at the beach with Irene
before the shoreline vanished
and the undertow of double-dipped sorrow
swept
her
away.

Janet is next in line.
She is about to bleed out her budget on
the med copay
for a blood thinner
derived from rat poison.
She fears one night the side effects
will leave her scratching at walls of isolation
in a frantic search to find
her misplaced medical alert bracelet.

Carol encourages her to make peace
with her medicine.

"It's less expensive than other anticoagulants and very safe."

She adds, "I love your earrings."

"Oh, thank you, a birthday gift from my daughter."

Next in line is Sam,
a well-groomed man in his seventies.
I can't help noticing the thumb on Carol's right hand.
It is extended upward as she gives him
his prescription of happy pills
for droopy
libido.

Pharmacological sign language for "go for it," perhaps.

Wait a minute.
What if I'm wrong about Carol?
It wouldn't be the first time I've misdiagnosed
a person's character.

What if Carol is really a dominatrix
who flogs millionaire vegans
with frozen clumps of kale
on her days off?

What if she is part of a conspiracy
to buy and hoard gallons of distilled water
to decrease the population of elderly with sleep apnea
causing the death of their dreams
next to parched CPAP machines?

No, no, I don't believe that.
Not for a second.

Who is Carol?
An angel?

Something better, I think.
A real human being.
The kind who feels
and cares
and gives
you that extra mile smile
when you need one.

I forgot that such people exist.
I'm glad they are still among us.

I hope someday I can be one of them.

Art Echo

You can lose your voice,
become the echo of others.

You'll blend.
They will like you.
You are now one of them.
You've identified.

They will nod in recognition
that you have finally seen
the dim light of their numb
neon vision of the human stage.

The bland leading the bland.
The soundbites of the toothless.
Don't join them.
Resist the dumber downs raising you up.

They will give you a voice,
then slit your throat
with the dull
cutting-edge
cutlery of conformity.

Sock Value

Every twenty-two minutes in America,
another sock loses its mate.

Somewhere between wash and dry,
somewhere between the last cool down
and first heated rotation tumble,
another linen,
another nylon,
suffers loss in the gain,
washes away in the tide.

Toe and sole mates separated, maybe for life.
From one-size synthetic to high-heel mohairs.
From heavy ply yarn to lightweight cyclist olefins.
Nothing can cushion the impact of this calamity.

"I lived with Fred's athlete's feet for two years,"
says a solo white anklet tennis sock,
 "but being alone like this is the worst."

Even cottons and wools,
accustomed to absorbing moisture,
find it difficult to absorb
the loss of their hosiery better halves.

"I've lost 50 percent of my support system,"
sighs a single red spandex.
"I don't know if I can walk through this alone."

A shrink-resistant, stretch fiber feels especially useless.
"I stayed up on Larry's leg and never once fell down.
I hugged those legs and feet through two loveless marriages.
Now what?"

Mr. Lee, the fifty-something Korean gentlemen,
who runs this laundromat,
is not unsympathetic to the plight
of abandoned footwear in front of him.

"I wish there was a government 'No Sock Left Behind' policy,
but there is none."

However, for business reasons, Mr. Lee maintains a six-day
discard policy for everything in the "Adopt the Sock Basket."
An elite one there cries, "I'm Nike, they can't discard me.
Even the Humane Society holds lost pets for seven days."

"Put a sock in it, Nike," yells a solo leg warmer.
"We're not dogs or cats. We're socks.
People don't bond with polyester.
They think we're just inert atoms with no feelings.
But they're wrong. They're so wrong."

A woman in her twenties enters the laundromat.
She asks Mr. Lee, "Did you find a thermal sock? I'm missing
one?"

Sure enough, the hollow core thermal
is found and immediately claimed.

"The winter ones usually find a home," sighs a quarter top.

"And to think I once complained about being used as a puppet,"
says a solid black antistatic.

"I'm barely holding on by a thread," shares a slipper sock.

Leave it to the frayed, over-the-knee, ultra-sheer, light support
to come up with an over-the-top
life-affirming word on the last day.

"Hey, I don't know about you guys, but I've got no regrets.
The run in my hose testifies that I finished the race."

"Hey, ultra-sheer, you just knocked our socks off,"
said a wool midcalf.

"They think we're just inert atoms with no feelings,"
polyester says again, "but they're wrong. They're so wrong."

Remembering Mary

In the end, maybe it doesn't matter
that they never wrote back
that he didn't apologize
that the salsa stain
on your cardigan
never came out.

That your dreams
fell asleep in the womb
that you were often passed over
passed by
and never learned to conjugate
verbs in the past-perfect.

That you lost your will to live
but kept on living
failed geometry twice
never did vegan, never did Vegas
never did what they told you
never told them what you did
never got what you deserved
never deserved what you got.

That you flossed twice a day
took your blood pressure meds regularly
watched your sodium intake
and the nightly news

once snoozed three Facebook friends
never saw Elton John perform live
or viewed Lenin's dead body.

In the end, what does matter
is the day when Mary's DNA
pressed the SELECT ALL option
on the keyboard of her cerebellum
then its index finger on the DELETE KEY
making one last withdrawal
from Mary's memory bank.

Maybe it does matter
how two days after that
Mary's husband Bernie sat at the table
with a half-eaten English muffin
and a Kodak moment photo of their summer
vacation in the Cotswolds decades ago.

He reminded Mary of a pub
where they dined on Sheep Street
how the One who is able to restore
the heavenly manna of memory
will, in the end, make all things new
even perhaps offering them
a platter of bangers and mash in Paradise.

At that moment
Something lit up
in the dark hallways
of Mary's hippocampus.

After not speaking a complete phrase
in sixteen months
she suddenly blurted
"Bangers and mash?
I had almost forgotten
how much I loathe that dish."

Mary never spoke again.

At the church,
during Mary's brother's solemn eulogy
Bernie remembered
his wife's last words
and broke out
in what some described
as unholy spasms of laughter.

It was an awkward moment, to be sure
but Bernie didn't care.

In the end, he reasoned
maybe it doesn't matter
if there's bangers and mash
in Paradise.

He'll have Mary again
and hopefully
some decent Chinese takeout.

White Noise

My wife has trouble sleeping at night,
so I went to shop for a white noise machine.

They say the sound of white noise drowns out
unwanted background noise to produce
an unobtrusive environment at night.

A whoosh sound, not a wuss.
That's a different sound.
Although that can be a white noise too.

So when I asked the Black manager
at the mattress shop
if they carried white noise machines,
he gave me a quizzical look.
I felt that we both understood the irony of my inquiry.

My wife needs a white noise machine
to get a better night's sleep.
Perhaps, for this man,
white noise has kept him
and his ancestors
awake at night
for centuries.

What does white noise sound like to a Black person?
Like a crowd at Nascar?
Hockey skates on ice?
A Tea Party rally?
The rustling of a Confederate flag
at the South Carolina capitol building?
"White Christmas"
piped into a miniature Christmas village,
like the one in *It's a Wonderful Life*?

The only Black person you see
in Bedford Falls is Lillian Randolph,
the Bailey family's maid.
Lillian Randolph had a wonderful life.

I meet a lot of Black people
who seem to have wonderful lives.
Maybe not according to some
white noise people's standards,
but they look happier
than many white noise people I know.

One white noise sound
on a white noise machine
is "Summer Nights."

I remember living in NYC
and most of my summer nights
included bongo beats after midnight,
police car sirens,
and occasional gun shots.
I recall sleeping pretty well
despite those urban tonalities.

"Ocean Sounds" is another offering
on a white noise machine.
When I hear ocean sounds,
I think of the body of another prostitute,
washed ashore on a Long Island beach,
and a serial killer on the loose.

I'd make a lousy white noise machine salesman.
My selling points aren't slumber friendly.

"I know what you're talking about,
but we don't sell those machines,"
the Black manager says to me.

I bet he went home that night and told his wife
about the white noise machine guy
and they laughed
themselves to sleep.

Lonelier Than

Lonelier than a pillow without a dream
Lonelier than an excuse without an attempt
Lonelier than a vanity mirror without a movie star
Lonelier than a pecan without a pie
Lonelier than a lover's knot without a beau
Lonelier than a flag without a country
Lonelier than a canyon without an echo
Lonelier than eyebrows without a surprise
Lonelier than a calendar with no invites
Lonelier than a census taker on Jupiter
Lonelier than a frame without an image
Lonelier than a seamstress at a nudist colony
Lonelier than a wedding ring on a widow's finger
Lonelier than a thought without a feeling
Lonelier than a poem without a reader

Remote Romance

We share the same remote,
but lately we are not on the same channel.

The **On Demand** button
is stuck with fig jelly
I spilled last week.
I don't feel I have the right
to demand much anymore, anyway.

The **Select** button also has OK written on it,
but things are not that OK,
so I'm not selecting anything.

I pressed the **Last** button last week and saw us
in lobster bibs in some Florida seafood restaurant decades ago
looking very much in love and eager
to get our claws into each other.

Whenever I press the **Info** button,
a line stretches across the screen:
"Come out of yourself, you pathetic narcissist."

You know what?
That's something you'd expect from the **Set Up** button,
but I think all these buttons are setting me up for failure.

I stopped using the **Input**, **Menu**, and **Guide** buttons.
I refuse to put my fingerprints
on the weapons of my own character assassination.

I can't explain why
the **Help** button instructions
show up in Bulgarian.
I didn't know Bulgarians
needed instructions.

We watch a lot of reruns these days.
We already know what's going to happen in each episode,
but we remain focused like we're watching for the first time.

It's familiar, but oddly engaging.
Maybe that explains a lot about long-term relationships.
But who am I to say?

According to the **Info** button,
I'm just a "pathetic narcissist."

However, tonight is different.

While watching the World War II
episode of the allies bombing Berlin,

led by the highly decorated
Jewish-American pilot
Lieutenant Colonel Robert Rosenthal,
my wife and I
hold hands.

I can't exactly say why,
but while witnessing the fall of Fascism,
the two of us connected
like we hadn't in a long time.

Tomorrow night we're going to watch *Patton* together,
then go out for dinner.

I know a great place for lobster.

Figs

The days merge into each other.

Tuesday thinks it's Wednesday.
Thursday knows it's garbage day,
so it points to the calendar to acknowledge its importance,
as if to say to Friday and Saturday:
"I've always lived in the shadow of your weekend social life.
No one ever says to me, 'Thank God, it's Thursday.'
How does it feel to be just another day like me?"

Meanwhile, my hair grows.
My patience recedes.
I read Turkish obituaries in English.

I have a lot of time for different things now.
I discover that an Ahmed Bahar in Ankara died of the virus.
Ahmed was in the food export business to America.
Dried fruit. Figs and apricots.

My whole body is shaking now.
Maybe Ahmed sold figs to Trader Joe's.
I ate four Trader Joe's Turkish figs last night.
What if Ahmed sneezed,
coughed,
touched,
or even looked at those figs?
I'm a dead man.

Wait a minute.
Hold it.
This is CAD—Corona Anxiety Disorder.
I can't go there.
I just need to take a deep breath and calm down.

Should I Skype, Zoom,
or FaceTime
with someone?

No. I resist technology's prophylactic promise
to impregnate our collective isolation.
I check my emails instead.

I click on an auto parts ad.
They offer brake pads,
spark plugs,
alternators,
water pumps,
curbside service,
free delivery,
free pick up,
and, get this,
a free made-in-house tofu curry salad sandwich.
On June 12.
One day only.

I forward the auto parts ad to all my contacts,
inviting them to the event.
We need to support this business.
Think about it—an auto parts supply place
offering a free curry tofu sandwich.
What better way to bring us all together at such a time as this?

I feel so encouraged.
Nietzsche would mock my newfound positivity,
but this is the same guy who didn't share
his marzipan cookies with Helga Schmidt
on their first and only date to the movies.
It was a Fritz Lang double feature.

Anyway, I am so pumped for this June 12 event.
For sure, I need to be extra diligent
to protect myself from the virus.
Wash hands.
Sanitize countertops.
Resist touching my face.
Wear mask.
And, above all, avoid reading
Turkish obituaries.

Obstructed Views

We grew up in the Philly area, and the most fun I had as a youth was going with my dad to see the Phillies and, in those days, the A's play baseball at Shibe Park.

The stadium was in a bad neighborhood, and when you parked, tough-looking entrepreneurial kids would ask if they could watch your car while you were at the game. It was extortion, of course, but this was Lehigh Avenue and, hey, that's baseball.

Climbing the steps to the stadium, we got hit with the aroma of ten-cent cigar smoke. Peanut shells crushed under our feet like moth larvae. Metal beams holding up the upper deck created an obstructed view of everything, unless you sat in the box seats, which we seldom did.

My life back then was filled with names like Ashburn, Ennis, Burgess, Robin Roberts, Musial, Snider, Koufax, Podres, Gus Zernail, Bobby Shantz, and a catcher named Joe Ginsberg. I asked my dad if Joe Ginsberg was related to us. He looked at me funny and laughed.

When the Yanks came to town, I saw Mantle, Mize, Ford, Berra, and Rizzuto.

Sunday double headers were the best: an all-dad day.

Sometime later, the A's moved out of Philly to Kansas City. I moved out of the house to go to school in New York.

My dad and I grew apart.

When he died, I didn't get there for him.

He died alone.

We didn't talk much at the games. We kind of gave signs to each other, like third-base coaches give to runners on second in scoring position.

But I think he knew.

This was the best it would ever be between us.

And he was right.

That Night

On the night John Lennon was shot,
I was two blocks away
getting a hot dog
and a drink at Gray's Papaya stand
on West 72 Street and Broadway.

I heard what I thought were two gunshots,
but nobody seemed to react.
Maybe they didn't hear it,
or maybe they pretended not to.

I finished my drink and ran with my hot dog to the action.
I saw a frantic Asian woman and a man with a bloody white shirt
being placed into what looked like an unmarked police car.

I always stopped at the papaya stand to get a drink
before I began my midnight shift as a doorman across town.
When I got to work,
I told Musli, the Albanian guy I relieved at the door,
that John Lennon had just been shot.

"Who?" he asked.

He didn't know who Lennon was.
I couldn't blame him.
Musli was a guy who saw Nazis
burn down homes and
throw babies into fire.

He taught history in Tirana until Communist
authorities told him he could not talk about God.
That night he fled with his family to Greece
and eventually found his way to America.

He never adjusted to life in the new land.
One time the guys at work sent him to get a pizza.
We watched him carry the box down the street sideways,
with sauce and cheese leaking onto the sidewalk.

"Who?" he asked again.

"Oh, some rock star," I said.

After you've seen babies thrown into fire,
there isn't much left to
imagine.

No Matter What

I will stay true, no matter what
I will love, no matter what
I will not fear, no matter what
I will believe, no matter what
I will not be silent, no matter what
I will not lie, no matter what
I will not quit, no matter what
I will make peace, no matter what
I will hope, no matter what
I will forgive, no matter what
I will trust, no matter what
I will pray, no matter what . . .

"Really," a voice replies

You are too weak
You are too old
You are too selfish
You are too needy
You are too impatient
You are too vain
You are too soft
You are too hard
You are too wounded
You are too fearful
You are too proud

And I say to this voice:

"What?"

"No matter"

Howdy

My eyebrows no longer rise to the occasion.
The element of surprise is missing.
The two furry ridge twins of tedium
have little reason these days
to elevate, celebrate, or levitate.

I don't blame them.
I don't give them a lot to work with.

It's not that I have seen it all,
it's as if all that I've seen is not enough.

They are waiting for something— anything—
to cause them to go vertical again.

Tonight, while surveying the restaurant menu,
they hope for some upward mobility,
that I will order something
less safe, familiar, and heart healthy
for a change.

But they know I will probably refuse
the shellfish and choose the broiled salmon
with steamed broccoli
to appease my cholesterol-stricken conscience.

They sulk all night,
even through the fruit salad.

Yesterday, while getting a haircut,
Melanie asked for permission
to trim my eyebrows.
They had grown like an untended forest
in a land of fixed foliage.

I paid for the $13.00 haircut with a twenty-dollar bill
and told Melanie to keep the change.

Her eyebrows lifted like Howdy Doody's eyebrows
when he captures the elusive magical cowboy hat
and becomes a rodeo star.

While driving back home,
I recalled a shellfish experience
I once had in Maine.
I ate three lobsters
in one sitting
with tons of melted butter.

That same year I had a heart attack.

I think about Howdy Doody,
his amazing bronco-riding skills.

Howdy now resides at the Detroit Institute of Arts.
His eyebrows are still raised.

A Poem on Valentine's Day

So, I get there.
Oh my, heaven.

Nobody says the word *pastiche* up here,
and nothing is for sale, nothing.
Free, everything is free, and I'm free.

And there's Moses eating quiche with ham and cheese.
And I'm thinking, that's not kosher.
But he says it's different up here.
"Better," he says, "better."

And I feel, oh my, I made it.
I made it. I'm here.

And there's ping pong.
The prophets are playing ping pong.
Isaiah with a slam that leaves
Jeremiah in hysterical laughter.

Surprise: Some people wear glasses,
which is an inside joke
because nobody needs them.

Also, no in-groups.
Everybody has equal access to God

at all times,
and it's less crowded than I thought.

That's because a lot of people
on the weekends take off to summer homes
on Saturn and Pluto,
or to visit galaxies that have bed and breakfasts
where all amenities are included,
even though nobody eats or sleeps much up here.

And I'm so happy now,
happier than I ever was on earth.
God, and Jesus, the angels,
and I'm meeting all kinds of delightful people.

And lots of clubs you can join.
I am learning Farsi, well, 'cause I have time.
I especially enjoy Isaac Newton's Thai cooking class.

And I don't miss anything on earth.
But you . . . I miss you.

They say after a while up here
you get over those feelings.
But I don't think I will get over you.

In a million years,
maybe two million,
maybe after I learn how to make
a shredded chicken lettuce wrap.
Maybe then.

Or as they say in Farsi, *īn nīz bogzarad*:
"this too shall pass."
I'm not sure I said that right.
Missing someone you love
is not easy to express
in any language.

Even if you have forever.

How to Handle Rejection

It always starts the same way: "Thank you . . . We regret . . ."

I'm so accustomed to these emails that I now write my rejections for the editors. I feel a need to relieve the anguish these poor people go through when rejecting a writer's work.

This morning I sent an email to Mark, assistant editor at a snobby academic poetry journal.

"Phil, thank you for submitting. We had over three hundred submissions and it was a difficult decision process. Besides, you should be used to rejection. Even your high school guidance counselor didn't offer you much hope of success in life. Keep writing what's in your heart and watch your sodium intake."

It's been a month since I sent that email to myself.

Still no word from him.

Just what I needed.

More rejection.

Size 41

My weary wardrobe hangs
in the gallows of my closet,
a naked reminder
that I too am no longer
in fashion.

Tweeds and wool,
cords and flannels,
summer blazers,
and winter suede,
a host of disembodied haberdashery
that once clothed my ambitions.

All of them are pleading with me
for one more night out.
I tell them they are wrinkled
and without buttons.

They remind me that they carry
the stains of the last fifteen years.

A black suit with moist sleeves
worn at my brother's funeral.

A seersucker jacket that endured
a blind date with a girl who saw right through me.

A red Christmas cardigan two sizes too cheerful.

After I close the closet door,
they will talk about their glory days
at Gimbels, Macy's, and Saks,
and how they never thought
they'd end up in a thrift store,
and how they once clothed bankers
and lawyers
and even a Hollywood director.

They live with their labels.
I live with mine.

Willie Nelson and the Peloponnesian War

In my dream, I'm hiking.
I don't even know why I'm hiking.
I don't want to be outdoors.

What am I doing here?
For me, outdoors has bad associations:
World War II,
the Titanic,
Jerry Katz's wedding.

All tragedies.
All outdoors.

Oh no. Now what?
What's that sound?
An animal?
No, it's water,
water coming from higher ground
to my feet.
First a stream,
now a flood.

This is it.
I'm going to drown in my dream.
What does it mean
to drown in a dream?

Never mind.
I don't have time for interpretation.

I'm in the water now,
but I'm not drowning.
I'm being carried downstream
into the arms of Maria,
a widowed Athenian umbrella maker
who lost her husband
in the Peloponnesian War.

She's listening to Willie Nelson sing
"It's a Dream Come True."
She says I am the answer to her dream.

Suddenly, I have the urge to pee.
The dream is interrupted.
When I return to bed, all is gone.
The dream and Maria.

All that remains are the usual existential questions:
What is the Willie Nelson-Nashville connection
to the Athenian-Spartan conflict?

The Peloponnesian War lasted twenty-seven years.
Thucydides, the ancient Greek historian,
wrote extensively about the war
between Athens and Sparta.

He never once mentioned Willie or Nashville.
He did mention that Spartans had a particular
weakness for pesto potato salad
with parmesan breadcrumbs.

And I know I didn't dream that up.

One More Day

What would you do if you knew you had just one more day?
Would there still be time to make amends?
Bid a last goodbye to friends?
Make peace with those who were your foes?

What would you do, what would you say?
If you knew you had only one more day?

Who would you give one last kiss?
Who would you most really miss?
Who would be there to hold your hand?
Talk to you of a Promised Land?
Who would be there to even share a prayer?

One more day is not enough
to learn all that quantum physics stuff,
or how to make a real baked ziti,
catch a sunset in Tahiti,
finally learn how to parallel park
before everything just fades to dark,
leaving perhaps with regret,
with no time left for one last laugh,
or even to get Jennifer Lawrence's autograph.

What would you do if you could live each day,
waking up happy just to begin it?
What would you do if you found a way
to release from your heart all the love that is in it—
every minute?

What would you do, what would you say,
if you could live your life unafraid every day?
That out of the broken sky came an answer
and you knew at last you found
a way to dare to trust and start anew?

What would you do? What would you say?
If you knew you were given just one more day?

In Search of Beauty

While asleep, a woman's voice in the night tells me I have the potential to be a beautiful person.

"Me?" I ask. "I think you have the wrong guy."

"Give it a try," the voice insists.

I wake up two hours later determined to beautify the world.

Driving to the respiratory supply place, my sense of beauty confronts a guy in a red pickup with angry hair.

He tailgates me so closely that it feels like a country western colonoscopy.

I want to rip his head off and feed it to a flock of East Texas albino crows.

I don't think that qualifies as a beautiful thought, so I cut and paste and save it in my frontal cortex clipboard for another time.

As he passes me, he gives me the look of a man more at home on a gun range than someone you'd meet at an Indian vegan buffet.

He gives me the finger. Thankfully, not his trigger finger.

I immediately draw on the beauty default settings in my

subconscious archives to avoid passive aggressive responses—should we meet at the next stoplight.

I conjure up Janet, the flight attendant with hair like a lemon cotton candy tornado, from which fly hummingbirds with lapis lazuli lips that harmonize a Bolivian folk song about an armadillo who couldn't make music until he died, and then his shell was turned into a beautiful instrument given to the most skilled musician in the land to play.

I want to share that story with the guy in the red pickup, but he's blaring Garth Brooks singing "Friends in Low Places."

I'm wondering if this guy ever participated in a Serbian spelling bee as a kid, and if Garth Brooks ever played in Bolivia, and if the lady on the GPS knows if there is a restroom nearby because I have to pee real bad and she tells me the nearest urinal is at the buffet restaurant two miles on my left.

She rebukes me for not peeing at the respiratory supply place, and casually mentions that prosciutto can be used in an antipasto but doesn't go well as a substitute for a knee replacement.

Real beauty, she adds, can be found Friday nights at the Rose Room Karaoke Bar in Anchorage, Alaska.

Ever Since The Fall

Have you noticed?
Ever since The Fall, people use deodorant.
Most people, anyway.

Ever since The Fall, people cut you off at intersections.
Meat companies put sodium nitrates in hot dogs.
Purses get lifted at restaurants.
Kids play with matches.
People cheat at poker.
Ankles get twisted.
Vows get broken.
Retinas get detached.
The water turns cold in the middle of a hotel shower.
Race cars plow into spectators.
Your boss micromanages your every move.

Ever since The Fall,
we've been trying to get back to what
we lost.
A sense of place, perhaps.
Hey, ask John Milton.
(Not the John Milton who works four to midnight at the Motel 7.)

Some people think the Garden of Eden was in Rochester, NY,
so they move there only to discover
people in Rochester cheat at poker
and cut you off at intersections too.

Have you noticed?

Ever since The Fall, it's hard to find a sweet kiwi,
an honest man,
a reasonably priced dental plan,
a cure for Lupus.

The list goes on and to tell you the truth,
ever since The Fall I've been a little cranky.
Probably you too.

So maybe we should be a little more patient and understanding,
because we're all bonded with universal brokenness.

And one day in eternity, if we meet Adam and Eve,
we'll just take turns beating the crap out of them.

If I Wrote a Poem

If I wrote a poem about the tango,
would you dance with me?

If I wrote a poem about nature,
could we take a walk together?

If I wrote a poem about anger,
would you be mad at me?

If I wrote a poem about being happy,
would it make you smile?

If I wrote a poem about living,
would it make you afraid to die?

If I wrote a poem about the way I feel,
would it make you feel the way I do?

If I wrote a poem about nothing,
would you give it meaning?

If I wrote a poem that moved you,
would you travel around the earth to be with me?

Maybe I shouldn't put
pressure
on
you
to respond to my poems.

Some things are out of the question,
even though there's no harm in asking.

Ballad of a Jewish Cowboy

Folks want to know where I've been and where I go.
My boots tell a story of my history.
There's more to me than the eye can see.

I'm really just a simple guy,
who likes to camp and gaze at the unsullied sky.
And imagine the clouds are made of *matzoh* brie.
And imagine the clouds are made of *matzoh* brie.

I like to sit round the fire just *noshin*
on a freshly baked prune *hamantashen*.
And think about that gal from Idaho,
whose potato *latkes* not so long ago,
won my heart.

Until, *oy vey*, she woke up one Boise day with a start,
having a pastrami, tsunami revelation.
That I was just another moody, foodie,
Jewish cowboy with no solid foundation.
And now I'm left singing a song of woe.

(Chorus)
Love is like a *babka* baked by Franz Kafka.
And no matter how you slice it,
there's always a little taste of sadness.
And how some days even the best *nova* still can't get you over
what was, what is, and what might have been.

And how fate is like a *dreidel* spin and sometimes
you have take things on the *shin,*
like a soggy *kreplach* in a salty broth.

And how not all our wishes turn into *knishes,*
but I'll keep my mouth from a froth,
'cause as long as I have my horse and saddle,
my holster loaded for any battle that might come my way—
I'm free.

A Jewish cowboy's life on the prairie,
despite separating meat from dairy,
is the life for me.

And I know all it would take for you to be convinced
is waking up to the smell of a cheese blintz
over an open fire.
Ah, my heart's desire.

So this ballad of the Jewish cowboy of which I sing,
though it may sound a wee bit strange,
is a greeting that to all I bring.

Shalom on the range.
Shalom on the range.

The High Price of Gas

The gas pump is drilling me with questions:

Debit or credit?
Zip code number?
Car wash?
Receipt?

Four questions—I feel like I'm at a Passover Seder.

But it doesn't stop there:

What were you doing in Mr. Harvey's garage that night?
Why did you ignore Gloria's overtures of affection?
Why have you never adopted a child from Portugal?
Do you know even one gluten-intolerant person in Cambodia?
Did you as a kid steal loose change from your father's coat pocket?

I'm going to be late for work if this continues.

Next there are yes-or-no questions dealing with my personality:

It is in your nature to assume responsibility yes or no?
You help people while asking nothing in return yes or no?
You take pleasure in putting things in order yes or no?
You feel at ease in a crowd yes or no?

Yes, Yes, Yes, Yes . . .

Fifteen minutes later, I discover I'm an ENFP.
An Extroverted Intuitive Feeling Perceiving person.
It costs me $42.76 to discover who I am.

I finally arrive at work and tell my boss I'm quitting.
My life as a credit analyst is being wasted.
Studies show that ENFPs have a natural propensity for acting.
Jerry Seinfeld, Sandra Bullock, Jim Carrey—all ENFPs.
I want to do film, Broadway, maybe a sitcom.
Mark Twain and Charles Dickens were ENFPs.
I see an epic novel in my future.

At home I tell my wife I found a new direction for my life.
She has a large suitcase at her side.
She just returned from filling her gas tank at a Conoco station.
At the pump, she discovered she's an ISFJ.
An Introverted, Sensing, Feeling, Judging person.
James Madison, Mother Theresa, and George Bush senior—
all ISFJs.
"I'm wasting my life in library science," she informs me.

She's moving to Buenos Aires to study tango.
I try to reason with her that James Madison and Mother Theresa
would never have danced the tango together, but to no avail.
I tell her that we shouldn't be hasty.
We'll wait a week,
refill our tanks,

and get a third personality analysis
at a Phillips 66.

The Gathering

At the memorial there was no talk about life after death.
No mention of eternity,
where we go
when we're out of step with time
and trip into the next world.

God was not mentioned.
The irrelevant in the room.
And Jesus? God forbid.

So we mingle.
Share stories.
The air is filled
with bittersweet sentiment.

Life will continue
until the next memorial
for the next friend,
when we gather again
and pay our respects,
and willfully remain debtors
to bigger truths
not mentioned amid
the sliced turkey,
jalapeño Monterey Jack,
and mayo-suffocated coleslaw.

Plastic wrap silence
covers the inconvenient condiments.

Mortality hovers
like the hungry fly
buzzing over the brie,
regarded as a pest
that seeks to feed
on our fears.

In truth, mortality merely seeks
a safe place to land,
unfazed by the flickering hand
of the faithless,
to explain itself more fully.
Even in French, if necessary.

Fragile Vow

Oh, it's you, Again.
Didn't I tell you, Again?
I didn't want to see you, Again.

There you go, Again.

Seeking that unsutured wound within
and stitching me up
with threads of wire
barbed in guilt and shame—again.

It's what you do, I guess.

Nevertheless, not sure when,
one day every fragile vow,
by God's grace,
will be kept.

And all that's left
will be the shout
of amen, amen, amen,
again and again.

And again.

Phone Call

When the call came that my mother died,
I was watching the Phoenix Suns-Lakers game.
One minute left to play.
Charles Barkley shooting two foul shots.
Score tied at eighty-nine.

The doctor offered condolences.

Barkley missed the first foul shot.

The doctor failed to mention
that my mother wanted to die.
She stopped all food intake
two weeks before I got permission
to leave work and visit her in Florida.

She didn't have to die.
She wasn't sick.
She fell down, like old people do.

But this time she didn't want to get up.
Didn't have much to get up to.
She lost her taste for cheese blintzes,
seeking stray cats,
yelling at my father and
donut shop employees and
everyone at the condominium office.

She once got stuck in the condo elevator
and yelled for help.
Nobody came to her rescue.

Barkley makes the second free throw.
Suns up a point.

My mom wasn't very well-liked, you see.
She would probably be yelling now
at James Worthy
as he dribbles down court
looking to make a play
with forty seconds left in the game.

"Pass the ball to Scott, you schmuck. Get rid of it."

I talked to my mother while she was in a coma.
It was probably our best conversation ever.
She listened.
Didn't have a choice.
I told her I forgave her for everything,
even for putting Mopsie,
my favorite dog,
to death.

Unlike my mom,
Mopsie wanted to live.

Mopsie wasn't old.
She wasn't ready to give up
seeking stray cats.

"We did all we could to keep your mother alive,"
the doctor says.
"And by the way,
if they don't pass the ball to Perkins
and get a score in the paint,
the Lakers are going to lose this game."

I reply, "Ainge just fouled, did you see that?
Now Byron Scott has two foul shots
and the Lakers are going to go up a point."

When I was at the hospital
I prayed over my mother.
A Pentecostal orderly saw me
and joined me in prayer.
He laid hands on my mom's head
and commanded her to rise out of her coma.
I don't remember saying amen.

Lakers are up a point,
just like I told the doctor on the phone.
Kevin Johnson is bringing the ball up court.
He calls a timeout,

bypasses the huddle,
goes to the public address system,
and announces:

"I just want to say at this point in the game,
and in life,
that Blanche Ginsburg,
Phil Ginsburg's mother,
has passed.
Could we have a moment of silence, please?"

The crowd respectively complies.
Play resumes.
Lakers grit it out, winning 93-92.
It was a big loss for me that night—
the Suns game and my mom.

But I got over it.
The Suns made the playoffs that season.

Every year on my mother's birthday,
I send a card to Kevin Johnson,
thanking him for offering public condolences for my mother
whom he never met.

And I never knew.

God in the School of Grammar

It is sometimes difficult to understand God's use of grammar.

He leaves question marks where we hope for a declarative
sentence, puts brackets and parentheses around our desires,
perhaps to modify our yearnings.

He ends sentences with ellipses . . . as if his train of thought got
derailed, to prevent the 3 p.m. to Connersville from running
over a prostrate Indiana teenager with track-marked arms.

He often speaks in fragmented sentences that would have
aroused the wrath of Mrs. Nichols, my sixth-grade English
teacher (it didn't take much to arouse her wrath).

At times his use of adjectives is less than positive.
When he speaks in the passive voice it often sounds aggressive.

He uses exclamation points sparingly, at least in my life.
When he uses the future tense, I don't know what to expect.
Some days I feel he hangs the entire universe like a dangling
participle struggling with a loss for words.

But hey, who am I to question God's use of grammar?
I wouldn't know a prefix from a suffix.

I once had a wonderful pre-fixed dinner at a tavern in NYC.

But this I do know: We are all complex sentences created for meaning, and direct objects of his concern, and although at times we feel like subordinate clauses grasping for the subject and verbs that complete our existence, our story is still in the hands of the best editor in the cosmos.

Who, by the way, wrote a book that explains the meaning of life, which, sadly, few people read. As they say in heaven, where even angels don't use the *Chicago Manual of Style*, "Ain't that a shame."

Global Warming

It's 9 a.m.
I'm walking on the boardwalk
in Hollywood Beach, Florida
and a prostitute approaches me.

"Do you want to cool off?" she asks.

I'm thinking: *At last,*
I can have a conversation
with someone about global warming.

The fossil fuels industry,
I tell her,
opposes action to stop global warming.

She, in turn, tells me:
"Do you realize that as glaciers melt
and warming waters expand,
sea levels will rise
anywhere from eight inches
to two-and-a-half feet
over the next century?"

She continues:
"In Florida, it is possible that seawater
will advance inland
as much as four hundred feet

in low-lying areas,
flooding shoreline homes and hotels.
You see the Fontainebleau Hotel? Forget it.
In five years, I won't be able to work the lobby
because there will be no lobby."

I add:
"You're right, and even more.
Global warming will pose all kinds of health threats
to people in Florida.
For instance, look for an increase
in heat-related illness,
air quality issues,
and infectious diseases
like herpes and . . ."

Oops. Maybe I shouldn't have gone there.

"Anyway," I continue,
"Florida's seniors, people like me,
will be particularly susceptible to these effects."

There is a pause in our conversation.

"Do you want to cool off?" she asks again.

I tell her, "Lady, I'm not that hot.

Just ask my wife.
She'll tell you.
I'm not that hot."

Wednesday Morning

I wake up panicked. It's gone. It's gone.

I rush to the lost and found in a city made of yesterdays and a woman with green marble eyes tells me a man who looks like me just came in to claim what I am looking for.

"Didn't you ask for some ID?"

"He took two eggs out of his pocket, broke the shells, and made the yolks dance for me," she says.

I rip the buttons off my shirt and toss them in the air and they transform into six sequined Liberian women singing a medley of Estonian folk songs.

"Can the man claiming to be me do that?" I ask.

"Sir, I make $9.50 an hour and my husband Lou has leukemia, and many days I'm not myself. I'm sorry," she says.

I go back to sleep, wake up three hours later, and break two eggs to make an omelet for breakfast.

"I'm so beyond dancing for people," says one yolk.

Both yolks, now bleeding in a bowl, fear the hot butter abyss awaiting them.

"Be brave," I tell them.

"Screw you," one replies.

I deserved that, I guess.

While I eat, I think of Lou with leukemia and his long-suffering wife, and how we wake up some mornings scared that maybe that something, that someone, is slipping away from us, or that spending forever in a hot butter abyss with six Liberian singers in sequins could really happen.

I'm looking at my utility bill and wondering why it costs so much to find a little warmth these days.

I turn up the thermostat to seventy-four, thankful I don't live in a nudist colony in Iceland.

Or a city made of yesterdays.

Decomposting

I look for success stories about people
my age who became late bloomers.
I wonder if I will ever be one of them.
I'm not sure that will happen.

I remain like a perennial with potential.
Though planted,
fertilized,
watered,
repotted,
reseeded,
and placed year after year
in the light of the almost,
my roots go deeper and deeper
into the soil of buried breath.

I only want to be
a sweet fragrance in the nostrils of God.
But I might settle as a lavender air freshener
in some Omaha restaurant restroom.

If we should meet under such circumstances,
please be sure to first wash your hands
before you press and release
the balm of my aerosol sighs.

And please don't tell
any of my old friends
where you saw me.

They still think I am in a vase
plucked from the Garden of Eden
before The Fall
and kept in the home
of a Detroit high school janitor's kitchen window.

I have no idea who would spread
such an outrageous rumor about me.

Come to think of it,
maybe I did.

Nature Lover

I picture a sunrise.

Two lines into describing the sunrise, the sky is suddenly
darkened by a tornado that lifts Jenny Mae Warner's home forty
feet into the air, carrying away a picture of her late grandma
Pearl who once broke an accordion over her husband Leo's head
because he cheated on her with that low-life waitress Gloria
from the Savoy Diner.

And now the page is filled with rancid accusations and the
detritus of disquiet from the living and the dead, leaving the
cornfield a carnage.

So I apologize to Emerson, Frost, Hardy, Tennyson, Keats, and
all the great poets who could walk through the woods and never
muse for a moment about Lyme disease.

I guess it's not in my nature to fully appreciate nature.

But if you invite me to walk hand-in-hand with you, through a
mythical meadow amid the morning dew, well, of course, for
you, I'd do the dew.

Bodies Everywhere

Antibodies
Somebodies
Nobodies
Everybody
Body of Christ
Body of work
Body of water
Busy bodies
Body builders
Body suit
Body shop
Body check
Body guard
Body clock
Body odor
Body of lies
Body of deceit
And then one day
A body bag
Over my dead body
Waiting to become
A resurrected body
Thanks to the One
Who provided
A body of proof

Sugar Cone

I'm waiting for the end of the world.
Truthfully, my world ended forty years ago.

That was the day
I walked out of Mr. Mitchell's sweet shop
with a sugar cone scoop of chocolate ice cream
and the scoop fell out of the cone
onto the sidewalk.

I wanted to put the suddenly streetwise scoop
back into the cone,
but it was already covered
with the fecal footprints of history.

I could have complained
to Mr. Mitchell
that he didn't pack the scoop correctly,
but he had enough to worry about
concerning his daughter Barbara
and a certain geometry-challenged halfback
on the JV football team.

Since that day,
I have suffered a personal meltdown,
and every June 12
I wake at dawn
pointing an empty sugar cone to the sky

and commanding fire and brimstone
to be poured out on earth
to avenge the injustice of it all.

And every year, it's always the same thing:
No fire and brimstone ever falls.
Only rainbow sprinkles.

Success Pays a Visit

I don't need you now.
You're a little late.
I was ready years ago,
but you procrastinated.

Where were you?
Now it doesn't matter.
Do you even know what time it is?
Don't you understand?
You missed the deadline.
Why did you wait so long?

How did you even find me?
Was I referred to you?
Who referred me?

Where were you when I needed you?
Why did you exhaust my hope
until I became disfigured with indifference?

Do you really think I still need you?
I know, I know what you're going to say:
"I wasn't ready for you back then."
But why come now?
Do you even know what time it is?

I am ashamed to say
that I still need you.
You know that, don't you?

But be careful.
I might sabotage your plans for me.
I just might do that.

You're not that important to me now.
You got that?
Do you understand?

Where the hell were you
when I needed you?
No, don't go.
Don't go.

You hungry?
I've got pierogies in the freezer—potato and onion.
Stay, please stay.
Let's share a meal together.
Get to know each other.
All right? Okay? We're good?

We've both waited a long time for this.
Thank you for remembering me.
Where the hell were you
when I needed you?

The sour cream is moldy.
All I've got is applesauce.
You like applesauce?

A Night Out

It's 10:30 at night and I'm walking with my girlfriend toward 102nd Street and Central Park. I turn to her and say, "We're never going to make it to the end of the block."

Sure enough, two guys from the neighborhood approach us.

"Give me ten dollars," one says.

"No," I reply.

They're in front of us now. The same guy flashes a pistol from under his coat.

"Give me ten dollars or I'll blow your head off."

I'm in an existential situation: How much is my life worth anyway? Ten bucks seems awfully high. I always figured seven-fifty, maybe eight, tops. Meanwhile, my girlfriend is anxiously rummaging through her purse.

I know I have a twenty-dollar bill in my wallet. The thought occurs to me: What if I give him the twenty? Do I ask for change? It would make a great story, but I probably wouldn't live to tell it.

Now my partner hands them a ten-dollar bill. They seem satisfied and leave.

We keep walking. A few minutes later, we're telling the story to my girlfriend's parents.

"We just had a gun pointed in our faces."

"Were you scared?"

"Sure, we were scared."

"What did you do?"

"We stayed calm, did what they asked."

"Wow, you're both lucky to be alive."

"Yeah," I said. "We really are."

We went through a lot together, that girl and I, but we fought like crazy and broke up for good six months later. She never asked me to reimburse her for the ten dollars she spent that night to save my life.

Years later I thought of sending her a check.

For seven-fifty.

Could I Be Bob?

I came out of the supermarket and a guy I see at the gym once in a while nodded to me and said, "How you doin', Bob?"

And I drove home thinking: *Could I be Bob?*

Could I be Bob, the retired kickboxer who now runs a bike shop and hopes every day some punk with a pistol will come into the store and demand money so he can display his Muay Thai Art of Eight Limbs technique and leave this out-on-bail felon bloodied and broken next to the bash guard of a BMX with four-to-six inches of front suspension?

Could I be Bob, the pastor who prophesied the world would end in fire in 2002 and the new heavens and new earth would begin on May 12 that year, and that the only sign left of previous civilization would be a burned-out shoe store in Minneapolis?

Could I be Bob, the supermarket produce guy who everyday sifts through asparagus spears and hurls darts of displeasure at his mother-in-law who wants him to put down the dill and exert his will and bring home more bacon for her daughter Jenny who's a dollar store shopaholic?

And could I ever be Bob, who performed the Heimlich maneuver on a seventy-six-year-old former district attorney choking on an artificial parsley-flavored crouton at a salad bar who, unbeknownst to Bob, would suffer a massive coronary three days later at home while playing Scrabble with his wife of fifty-two years who just finished making the word *classic* worth twenty-one points?

I don't think I can be Bob. I'm just me.

I wish he had called me Steve.

I could be Steve.

Another Day in the Dictionary

A fight is about to break out between pages 102 and 103 in my dictionary.

Ballistic is hurling insults across the binding at balsamic.

"Look at you, you wimp of a word. I mean, what do you do? Eh? You hang out with red lettuce and you've got friends with names like radicchio, chard, and arugula."

It's to be mentioned that no other words on page 102 want to see violence. Ballad, balloon, and ballerina are trying to reason with ballistic. Ballot wants to take a poll to see who's in favor of conflict.

But ballistic will have none of it.

"What am I doing on the same page with you, jellyfish?" he says. "Who are you calling a jellyfish?" comes a voice from page 804. It's the voice of jellyfish.

Now this altercation is in danger of spreading across seven hundred pages.

You don't want the Js involved. They've got javelin, jugular, and judgment, not to mention Jehovah.

Meanwhile, balsamic has broken a twelve-year-old bottle of Trebbiano and Lambrusco syrup and is threatening ballistic with knife-like movements. Ballistic is armed with a projectile missile that, if fired, could do damage far beyond page 103. The fallout could reach mariachi and marinara.

Back on page 103, balmy, baloney, and banana are doing their best to restrain balsamic. Thank God for ballyhoo, who is disarming everyone with self-deprecating humor.

"What is all the ballyhoo here?"

"Hey, you with the missile, are you going ballistic?"

Even ballistic can't keep a straight face.

Ban now gets up and reminds everyone that there's a treaty between pages 102 and 103. And that words have power, and that sentences of mass construction could wipe out our entire lexicon. They are dictionary words, he reminds them. Each has its own definition and dignity of space.

They aren't living under a thesaurus tyranny like hundreds and hundreds of fellow words, who everyday inhabit unspeakable, cramped, unalphabetized paragraphs arranged in alien categories and forced into abstract relations with indeterminate numbers.

At this point, banal is yelling, "Here, here!"

Nobody on either page pays attention to him.

Now something unpredictable is happening: All the words on pages 102 and 103 join together in the binding, including even balk, who never wants to do anything.

Bake is giving out cookies. Balderdash is telling jokes. Bald is showing off a new hairpiece.

Everyone agrees that the battle is not with each other but with a world that now prefers visuals. Let us not forget that "in the beginning was the Word." Everyone looks encouraged.

And from the balcony, baguette, grasping the sticky hands of baklava, yells an amen so loud that even zigzag and zither wake up and fall out of their beds.

Friends for Life

Everywhere I go loneliness goes with me.
I don't get it.
Doesn't loneliness have any friends?

Last week I tried to introduce
my loneliness to other people's loneliness
at a social gathering.

It kind of worked.
My loneliness went off to a corner
and seemed to have a lot in common
with the loneliness of others,
but that wasn't the case.

After we got home,
my loneliness told me
that he tried to bond with other people's loneliness,
but he still felt like an outsider.

"Now you know how I feel sometimes," I told him.

I have to admit,
loneliness is a faithful
companion in my life.
Always there for me,
even if I don't acknowledge him.

Independence Day is coming,
and loneliness wants to know
what we are doing.

"I have no plans yet," I tell him.

"What about New Year's Eve?" he asks.

"Too far ahead to think about," I reply.

"Well, whatever happens, I'm here for you," he says.

"I know," I tell him.

I once tried moving to another city
to leave my loneliness behind.
Two days after I arrived,
I discovered loneliness
had tagged along with me.
I was kind of relieved.
After all, I didn't want to feel
all alone in a big city.

Tonight, at dinner,
loneliness reminds me
that I didn't receive phone calls today.

"People are busy," I tell him.

We watch a Yankees game together
and go to bed.

Loneliness and I
might not have everything in common,
but we both like sports.

Brown Spot

My brother had a brown spot on his back
when he was a teenager.
Over the years it got bigger and browner.
He rubbed it and it bled.
And then one day we found out it was melanoma.
At age thirty-one, it killed him.

My parents were devastated.
My brother was the constellation of the family.
He was a lawyer,
then a judge,
one of the youngest in the state.

I knew what my parents thought.
Why him? Why not the other one?
Why him, who made us so proud?

Even I said, "Why him?"
It should have been me.
It's the black sheep who deserves the brown spot.

But after my brother died,
I found some stuff buried in his closet.
Stuff judges put people in jail for.
Pictures of women,
the kind you see in bondage magazines.
The stuff my brother was into on weekends

would have killed my parents
if they had known.

I burned those pictures
in a pot one night
in the backyard.
All my brother's bondage
went up in smoke,
like my parent's dreams.

Rash Decisions

Sometimes I want to crawl out of my skin.
But where would I go?

Crawling among humans in our culture is looked down upon.
Crawling without skin is not legal in Rhode Island.
Crawl into any three-star restaurant
without your skin
and I guarantee
they won't honor your reservation.

Of course, there is a better chance of finding loose change
when you're crawling.
But I don't need money that bad.

If I crawled out of my skin,
I don't think people would notice.
Most folks think I'm only skin deep anyway.

What about my skin?
Where would it go without me?
Eczema may be itching for independence,
but I don't see it holding a steady job.
I can't imagine hives on a dating site
getting beyond social anxiety issues.
I mean, what does skin do on its own?
Go skinny dipping?

People might ask me what color my skin was
before I crawled out of it.
Prejudice comes in many different colors.
It's a pigment of our imagination.

Don't you love people who say,
"He's so comfortable in his skin"?
Don't people like that ever feel failure,
humiliation,
rejection,
and disappointment?
What is wrong with them?

Well, I don't think I can crawl out of my skin.
I need to keep my dermatologist appointment next week.
I don't want my problems to affect someone's livelihood.

Besides, my dermatologist
accepts me
just as I am,
warts and all.

Ruler of the Rem

I have this dream that I'm in a room.
In the room is a red button.
Behind me is a large glass window.
This red button, if pressed,
will cause cataclysmic destruction
and annihilate the entire planet.

People behind the window frantically shake their heads.
They don't want me to press the button.
These are the same people who don't return my emails,
hang Thomas Kinkade paintings in their bathrooms,
and know all the right things to ask in hardware stores.

I'm still thinking about what to do.

Now the people behind the window are banging on the glass.
I haven't received this kind of attention before.
I'm not used to it.
But I'm thinking,
What would the end of the world mean anyway?

No more waxed nectarines,
Shanghai sweat shops,
partially hydrogenated oil,
or tanning salons.

So far, all I see are positives.

No more job insecurity,
high school cliques,
viscosity breakdown,
ice skating shows,
or E. coli cheeseburgers.

My index finger is getting hot.
The people of God won't mind if I press the button,
for glory awaits them.

But those people with unopened cans of nutmeg
and others who know
the secrets of tungsten will be upset.

Baby boomers with red convertibles
and yellow socks
will feel violated.

Zookeepers with sinus headaches won't mind,
but overpriced tax accountants
and people with "Save the Tilapia" bumper stickers
will take it hard.

Blue tango instructors,
Ukrainian fudge makers,
and Persian carpet cleaners
naturally have the most to lose.

Hey, that's life.
What are you going to do?

Anyway, I wake up and go downstairs to check my email.
I'm shocked.
No one has communicated with me during the night
even though the very life of the planet is at stake.

Tonight I will dream the same dream again.
The same people will desperately bang on the window.

Sometimes I feel uncomfortable having all this power.
But what can I do?

A man needs a dream
or it's not even worth getting up in the morning.

Missing Person

I was missing for three months before they found me.

"Where were you?" they asked.

"I was right here with you," I said.

"We didn't see you," they replied.

"That doesn't mean I wasn't here."

"Just because we see you now doesn't mean you're really here," someone else said.

After that I wore a tee shirt with my picture on it that read, "Have you seen me?"

I was amazed at how many people recognized that it was my face on the tee shirt.

"Isn't that you? You're not missing," a woman in the supermarket said to me.

I think I needed to hear that; however, I don't always wear that tee shirt.

Some days it's nice to be missed.

Inanimate Conversations

My friend gave me a barbecue spatula that talks.
It tells me when things on the grill are too hot or not done yet.
I passed by a house for sale the other day.
The sign read it was a "talking house."

I didn't grow up in a talking house.
My parents used up all their words before I was born.
But a barbecue spatula that talks gives me hope.
I want to fill my whole life with objects that converse.

A comb to tell me I have a nice haircut.
A water glass to remind me when I'm thirsty.
A handkerchief to tell me when to blow my nose or cry.
A chair that beckons me to sit.
Zippers that inform me when my fly is open.
Socks that whisper, "We don't match."

I need you to tell me that you love me
when things on the grill are too hot
or not done yet.

What's in a Name?

Corn syrup is being given a new name.
Who decides such things?
Did someone call a meeting?
Gather a staff?
Was corn syrup present when the announcement was made?

"We're giving you a new name."

"But all my friends—
fructose, glucose, dextrose, Karo—
they won't know me anymore."

"You're going to be called for what you really are—
oligosaccharide."

"Oligo? That's not who I am.
Everybody will make fun of me.
'Hey, Oligo. Oligo, amigo.'"

Corn syrup's not Italian or Mexican.
It's from the glucoamylase family.
I think it might be Welsh.

And saccharide?
It sounds so . . . well . . . Jewish.

"Oh, the Saccharides. You know what those people are like."

Why does corn syrup need a new name? Does this mean I have to stand behind corn syrup or Oligo at the DMV, waiting for it to get a new name on its driver's license? I never thought corn syrup should be driving anyway. It is always under the influence of the fungus aspergillus and drives too fast. Does this mean corn syrup will be online ahead of me at the Social Security office to make its name change? Aren't there enough bureaucratic delays in life without having to deal with corn syrup's identity issues?

If I changed my name, would it matter?

If tomorrow I took on a one-syllable, stronger, less-genteel, and more-gentile name like Clarke or Trent would my image change?

Would I suddenly have an overwhelming, uncontrollable desire to buy a rowing machine, do my own oil changes, play lacrosse, put mayonnaise on corned beef sandwiches?

What if everybody had the same name? It would be so much easier. All guys were Joe. All women, Ann.

What if Joe and Ann met on the street after not seeing each other for two years:

"Ann? Is that you?"

"Joe?"

It is said in scripture that the faithful will receive a new name from God. I dreamed such a dream one night. People came up to me in heaven and told me their new names.

"My new name is Virtue."

"My new name is Courage."

Someone asked me, "What is your new name?"

"Larry," I replied.

I think I'd prefer Oligo.

West 101 St. 1984

I'm walking back to my apartment and a street guy in the
neighborhood starts yelling at me.

"Did you see that? One of those Orthodox Jewish guys just went
in there. What's a guy like that going in there for?"

He's talking about the porn theater, which two months ago
was an art house for foreign films. It's a sign of the times, I'm
thinking. The screen that once refracted the faces of Yves
Montand and Catherine Deneuve now displays other parts of
anatomy, from the likes of Johnny Wadd and Fiona.

In two months, we've gone from the *The Seventh Seal* to *Anal
Island*. It's a sign of the times, all right.

But what about this Orthodox Jewish guy? What's he doing?
Did he take the train in from Williamsburg just to see this?

Like a bearded penguin in heat, he didn't bother to travel
incognito. He could have put on some Bermuda shorts and
dark glasses and arranged his hair in a ponytail. An East Village
pothead look would have drawn no attention. Couldn't he have
pretended to be a tourist from Tulsa? Carry a copy of *New York
on $40 a Day* and a bus schedule?

Maybe he's a diamond dealer who just ripped off his partner.
This is the last place his cohorts would look for him. Maybe he's

not an Orthodox Jewish guy at all, but some skinhead made up to look like one in order to embarrass the Lubavitch. Perhaps he's a drug addict who uses phylacteries to help him shoot up.

Or, more likely, he's just another fallen son of Adam, of Moses, of the tribe of Levi, of the descendants of Solomon, the wise man who had seven hundred wives and probably never sent an anniversary card.

It's August and *Insatiable* is playing.

None of us, even the most pious, is very satisfied with our lives.

Signs of the Times

I saw a guy with an Uncle Sam outfit
holding a sign advertising some income tax service.
I want a job like that—
costume, props, outdoors, get into character.

Theater.

I had an Uncle Sam.
He used to beat my Aunt Rose black and blue.
He ended up getting shock treatment
and turned out to be a nice guy.

Go figure.

The other day while driving,
I saw a guy dressed in a green bug outfit waving a sign.
I couldn't tell what he was selling—
maybe extermination services—
but the bug looked too happy to be promoting its own death.

Maybe the guy was pretending to be a bed bug,
rejoicing that no insecticide could kill him.
I wonder if bed bugs get insomnia or have sleep apnea.
I would trust a guy with a bed bug outfit selling mattresses.
Those creatures know mattresses.

Or maybe the bug guy's sign read,
"Be Nice to Lice Week."
So many causes, so little time.

I dreamed one night that I advertised the end of the world.
I wore this signboard around my neck stating,
"Repent the End Is Near"
and went about my day.

My daughter disowned me.

"My dad's got a brain tumor the size of a tennis ball."

My wife told friends, "His blood pressure is out of control."

The guys at the car repair place
installed a new timing belt but couldn't resist saying,
"This will last you another fifty thousand miles
depending on, well, you know
the eschatological timing of things."

I was impressed.
Guys at the brake shop
used the word
eschatological.

I told them,
"I'll be back in six months to get an alignment,
if the world's still here."

The woman at the barber shop
asked me to please remove the sign
before cutting my hair.
Usually talkative,
she said nothing
during my entire time in the chair.

She has dreams of opening her own salon.
I don't think I'll be on her mailing list.

I went to the mall.
The security guy stopped me and said,
"You can't advertise in here;
please remove your sign and leave."

I told him I was looking for a Roy Orbison CD
and wanted to get an Orange Julius.

"You must leave now," he said.

I wonder what John the Baptist would have done.

At the gym,
people on treadmills
kept giving me looks.
What's the point of getting into shape
if there's no world left to look good for?

I came home discouraged.
But I was surprised to find the Hebrew prophets
Isaiah, Jeremiah, and Ezekiel
sitting at my dining room table.

They shook their heads and said,
"You're going about this all wrong.
You need to be more in touch
with a postmodernist approach
to this kind of message."

Jeremiah suggested I change the words on my sign to
"World's Best Veal Cutlet Recipe. Ask Me."
I didn't know Jeremiah was into cooking and food,
especially Italian cuisine.

Ezekiel said, "Soften the message a little.
You might get better results."
He suggested,
"How about, 'Don't wait until it's too late to say I'm sorry.'"

English isn't his first language
so maybe his words read and sound
different in Hebrew.

I don't want to question Ezekiel—
he suffered a lot for bringing a message from God—
but after being in eternity for such a long time
I think he's lost his edge.

Isaiah (they cut him in half) told me,
"Try the car washes. You might get better results."

I had no idea what he meant.

"Repent the End Is Near."

I think people might receive that message better in other places,
like outside the cheesecake shop
where hundreds die daily from
slices of key lime swirl
which contain sixty-two grams of saturated fat.

Or Dhaka, Bangladesh
where the city dumps 9.7 tons of waste
into the river every year.

Or Khabarovsk,
Russia's coldest city,
where it reaches fifty-eight degrees below
Fahrenheit
and people's heads
turn into snow cones.

Or Linfin, China,
where breathing the air is like smoking
forty cigarettes a day.

Location, location, location.
Every message needs to find its location.

Next month I'm going to my fortieth high school reunion
in New Jersey.
The invitation arrived in the mail.
Would you believe,
"Repent the End Is Near" is the reunion's theme?
Apparently, I'm not the only one
God is speaking to in these last days.

Even so,
I'm torn between what entree to choose
for the Thursday night
"End of Days" reunion dinner.
Will it be the apocalypse pork loin?

The seven seals stuffed flounder?

I'm asking myself, *What would Jeremiah do?*
The flounder, I'm thinking.
Yeah, definitely the flounder.

The Showers

Heinrich Himmler takes a shower with soap
made from the flesh
of Marlene Rabinowitz's mother.

It's the closest
he will ever get
to intimacy
with a Jewish woman.

Marlene's mother,
twice violated
by the showers of the Shoah,
rests in the arms of Elohim.

Meanwhile, the sudsy
ex-chicken farmer
of Dachau
sings "Oh Tannenbaum"
joined by a choir of demons.

The Choreography of Corn

Corn on the stalk with bilingual ears
sway to the sound of workers singing
"Te Amo (Para Siempre)."

Most husks in the field
know this is the last dance.
Soon their lives will end up as side orders.
Some as an inharmonious hominy
placed alongside two fried, bleary-eyed, ocher eggs
in no mood for a morning marimba.

Others, perhaps destined to be frittered away
in the rancid rites of passage at Lil's Diner,
partnered on a blue plate
next to an embarrassed pork chop,
and forced to wear a pink,
confetti-like paper frill
around its charred bone.

Looking very much
like a cowboy
in a tutu
at a Laredo Masonic Hall line dance.

The Closing of The Crest

I'm sitting in The Crest cafeteria on West 57th Street.
The cafeteria will close in an hour, forever.
The Crest is my only reason to still live in New York
or maybe live at all.

Where else can I get a bowl of matzoh ball soup,
a brisket sandwich,
and blueberry blintzes
for a couple of bucks
every day?

Where else can my friends and I,
after smoking weed for two hours,
get hand-carved hot pastrami sandwiches
and a killer beef barley soup?

Then there's Gus,
the Venezuelan guy,
who works in the meat carving section.
He sometimes comes to my apartment
and smokes weed with us.

It's an honor to be in the presence of a gentile guy
who can slice corned beef
with the same skill
as a *mohel* performing a circumcision.

Roosevelt called Pearl Harbor
a date that shall live in infamy.
My heart sank deeper than the USS *Arizona*
on the day The Crest closed.
Roosevelt only had to deal with Japan.
I had to deal with the loss
of the best stuffed cabbage
I had ever eaten.

It's 8:30—a half hour left to closing.
I let my cheese blintzes,
soused in sour cream,
loiter on the plate
like a pair of backslidden drunks
in front of the Salvation Army.

For some reason,
maybe because the regular staff has already left,
the sweet Slavic woman,
who normally sweeps and mops the floor,
is being enlisted for her first and only
opportunity to serve food to customers.

Her countenance beams,
as if she had an epiphany and,
after gazing at the face of God,
descends from the Mount,

not with stone tablets in each hand,
but with plates of corned beef
and cabbage
and real mashed potatoes.

She serves a customer a hot turkey platter
that could feed a battalion
of Romanian soldiers.

I want her to adopt me.
Take me home.
Serve me dinner every night.

With fifteen minutes left before the eternal closing,
a homeless man enters
and gets a bowl of chicken noodle soup.

The Madame Defarge lookalike at the cash register,
a brittle, guillotine-jawed lady with a swastika-shaped soul,
realizes the homeless man has no money
and snatches the bowl off his tray.
He doesn't resist.

"Give him the soup! Give him the soup!"
I want to yell.
I want to pay for the man's soup,
but I only have a quarter.

"Give him the soup! Give him the soup!"

"It's the principle," she yells.
"It's the principle," she says again to herself,
her twisted integrity intact.

The homeless man goes back into the night.
Several staff begin to turn the chairs and tables
upside
down.

It's over for The Crest,
but I'm not finished with this cashier.
I imagine that,
at one minute to closing,
I approach her with Gus's carving knife
and eviscerate her gangrenous soul
amid the cheers
of the remaining staff and customers.

Fade to me
now on death row
in a pentobarbital
prone position.

"Any last words?" the warden asks.
"It's the principle," I reply.

"Now fry me
like the color of the breaded shrimp
at The Crest."

I'm Not Tofu

I'm not Tofu.

You can do anything you want with tofu.
That's what they tell me.
It has no real identity of its own.
Bake it, bread it, fry it, steam it, toast it.
Choke it, accuse it, ignore it, amuse it.
Read to it, teach it a skill, take it with you to Denmark.
Introduce it to pork.
Show it your birthmark.

I'm not tofu.

You can't do anything you want with me.
I'm a person. I have feelings.
I'm not just another cookie-cut chameleon.
You can't toss me in soy sauce
to be subsumed like some everyman.

You can do anything you want with tofu,
but I'm not tofu.

Except when I'm with you.
For you I'll be tofu.
You, and only you,
can do anything you want with me.
But you seldom do.

Assorted Centers

As a teenager,
I remember coming home
after a night out with friends.

The police were parked
in front of my house.

My parents had been fighting again
and someone called the cops.

One time there was candy
strewn all over the lawn.

My father's attempts at reconciliation
had ended with nougats
in the hedges,
butter creams
in the magnolias,
dark chocolate caramels
decomposing among the perennials.

I once found two
milk chocolate marshmallows
still in brown paper bunkbeds
huddled together
like a pair of runaways
from a foster home.

Our house had only one center.
It was always nuts.
Just nuts.

Ethnic Cleansing at the Pharmacy

I'm in the drugstore in Philadelphia.
What a shock to discover ethnic cleansing is available here.
There is actually a sign in aisle two that reads, "Polish Remover."

Polonophobia right here in Philadelphia,
the city of brotherly love.
Is there a pierogi pogrom going on?

This is like a revival
of the eighteenth-century
Prussian suppression of Polish people.

There is a mall not far from here.
Is it secretly a labor camp for Polish people?
Are there massacres taking place in the food court?
Are they deporting Polish people to New Jersey?

What we have here is the continuing
legacy of Frederick the Great.
He compared the Poles to the Iroquois of Canada.
But then again, Frederick's genitalia were harmed
by a cruel surgical operation to save his life
from an unnamed venereal disease.
Perhaps a Polish surgeon wounded him.
Maybe it's all a language problem.
I've been told the Polish verb *to be*
is pronounced exactly like *bitch* in English.

If you say *moze byc*, it means *it can be*
or *yes, that's okay.*
But half translated into English,
it means *it could be a bitch . . .*

That could result in some misunderstanding.
So when I complained to the cashier
about the "Polish Remover" sign,
and that the pharmacy was sending the wrong message,
she gave me a look of bewildered contempt and said,
"Polish Remover? That's *polish* remover?"

"Oh," I said, "Oh, yeah, right. I was just making a joke.
You know, like they say in Polish, *moze byc.*"

"What did you call me?" she said.

At that moment, I imagined being beaten
by ten pharmacy employees and
dying in the diuretics aisle
while humming
Chopin's "Funeral March" of *Piano Sonata No. 2.*

No One Believes Me

Growing up, we lived next door to the Castles.
These were really crazy people, always fighting.
One of them usually had a black eye.

Mr. Castle disappeared for over a year.
Nobody saw him.
Everybody assumed he was dead.

But I went to the racetrack
with my friend Steve Warner
and I saw Mr. Castle
at the trifecta window.

I went home and told my parents.

"Aaaa, you're nuts," they said. "Castle's dead.
And what were you doing at the racetrack with Steve Warner?"

Two months later,
Mr. Castle showed up next door.
Mrs. Castle made him a nice meal and then
banged a frying pan over his head.

This wasn't the first time my parents
didn't believe things I witnessed.
I came to Christ over forty years ago.

The second member of the Divine Trifecta
introduced himself to me in a California desert.

My parents
and a lot of friends
thought I had lost my mind.

"How can you believe such nonsense?"

"You're Jewish"

"What are you doing?"

I told them,
"I saw him, not with my eyes, but with my spirit."

"Aaaa, you're nuts."

"He's dead."

"Were you on drugs? Sure, you were on drugs."

I said, "He's alive and one day he'll return.
Just like Mr. Castle."

Just like Mr. Castle.

Goethe at Starbucks

If I told you my deepest struggles,
what would you do?
Would you be repelled?
Would you be surprised?
Would you judge?

Would you say you understood,
but in your mind
do a cartographer's remapping
of our emotional boundaries?

Goethe said, "Tell a person or else keep silent."
I tried to talk to Goethe about my issues,
but I don't speak German and he speaks little English.
Besides, he checks his email every ten minutes
and seems distracted.

I tell him about my soul's invaders,
how I'm often left with the carnage of my bad choices.
He reminds me of the invasion
of the Spoon Guards
of Napoleon's army
when they burst into his bedroom with drawn bayonets,
and how his wife Christiane
stood her ground and commanded them to leave.

I don't know how the conversation
shifted from my life to his,
but it was okay.

I paid for his mocha latte
and walked to my car in silence.

Recipes for Life

I went to the local bookstore the other day
and stopped at the food section.
They had a book of chicken recipes.
I like to cook.

Directly across from me was a book section on sexuality.
I noticed all the books high on the shelf.
Out of the reach of children, for sure.
Out of the reach of everyone.

Then I started thinking:

Is this why Wilt Chamberlain
the late seven-foot center
for the Los Angeles Lakers
reportedly claimed he was involved
with twenty thousand women?

He could have reached those books with no effort.

Short guys like me read about chicken,
which is okay.

My wife likes chicken.

Cosmic Cocktails

Have you ever heard the term *mixed blessing*?
Is that anything like a mixed drink?

"He got promoted to vice president of sales last month."

"Yeah, then yesterday he got laid off."

"Oooh, Piña Colada Punch."

"She finally got her Ph.D."

"Yeah, then she left her husband and ran away with the medieval history professor."

"Man, Flatliner."

"They had a great vacation on their twentieth anniversary until they got to St. Barts. Then she got stung by a stingray."

"Phew, Body Shot."

Life can be a capricious bartender, handing out mixed blessings like mixed drinks. One day you think you met the Tom Collins of your life and for a while it's Liquid Viagra and Thug Passion.

Then a year later, you wake up to a Tequila Sunrise and discover the Incredible Hulk was nothing more than a Fat Frog, Dingo who only wanted a Malibu Bay Breeze and Buttery Nipple, and now you're left feeling like a Surfer on Acid with a Rusty Nail in your soul.

But that's what some happy hours are like on this planet. Any one of us can go from a Strawberry Daiquiri to Russian Roulette quicker than Sex with an Alligator at a Baltimore Zoo.

Pass It to the White Guy

I'm playing basketball at the gym.
Nine Black guys and me.
Five minutes into the game,
and I haven't touched the ball.

My teammates are not passing to me.
It's not like they can't see me.

Three guys sitting on the sidelines offer me some feedback.

"They're not passing you the ball because you're White."

The second guy says, "It's 'cause you're short."

"It's because you're old," says the third guy.

I reply, "It's 'cause I'm Jewish."

Things aren't so black and white.

One Black guy on the other team is taking up my cause.
He yells to my team members:
"Why don't you pass it to the White guy?"

They do.

I take a twenty-five-foot
three-point shot
and it goes in.

I think I just proved
the existence of God
without a word.

Dream Life Invaders

I need a restraining order on people who keep appearing in my dreams uninvited.

An ex-pastor appears at least twice a week in my dreams to remind me that he died, went to heaven, and returned to earth to offer select people discount prices on his timeshare apartment in Paradise a block from King David's condo. I could tell it was another of those out-of-body real estate scams you read about on the internet.

Nicole Kidman shows up in my dreams at least once a week, offering me over-priced face creams guaranteed to make me look ten years younger. I asked her if she would go out with me if I looked ten years younger. She said she might consider it. I could tell she was just acting and didn't mean it. I bought the products anyway, just to get rid of her.

Then there's Phil Jackson, the former coach of the Los Angeles Lakers, who every so often berates me in front of the team for not hustling and getting back on defense. Of course, next year I'll be a free agent, but I might be dreaming that another NBA team will pick up my contract.

Oh, and how about this? Two nights ago, Mr. Duthie, my high school math teacher (the same Mr. Duthie who flunked me in algebra I and II) shows up in a dream. I asked him how he ended up in my dreams. He said he found me on "Limbic Links." For

$89.00 a year, this website offers a complete dream intrusion course called "From A to Zzzzs." And it's perfectly legal, except in Montana.

Well, my Mr. Duthie dream was harmless enough. He told me he wanted to play ping pong and about how his wife died and that whatever friends he had left were all restless sleepers who didn't dream much about anything anymore. He simply didn't have anybody else he could ask. I kind of felt sorry for him.

Besides, I went to summer school those two years and made up both courses. I understood the algebraic applications later in life, after I finally figured out y my x left me for another guy. I played him a game. Let him win. And then told him I had to go. I lied. You can lie in dreams. It goes on all the time.

The thing is, there's no dream invasion insurance. You can't put a pit bull around your subconscious, or a ring of fire around your REM. With dreams, you're just thrown into a story with characters you may or may not want to be with and who often react in uncontrollable ways.

Come to think of it, my waking life is a lot like that. Thankfully, not all my dreams are invasive. Some are heroic. The other night I dreamed I ran into a burning building to rescue people. I saved Nicole Kidman. I don't think she recognized me. Probably because I looked ten years younger.

August 12, 1952:
Dedicated to the Night of the Missing Poets

You've become one of them.
You once had a voice.
Now you're an echo,
in tune with the classroom conductors of conformity.
You have found the You in utopia.
Remember when you once lived among the outliers?
Found the truth in the margins.
You had a good view of it all from there.

What happened?
Why did you let them hit the tab button in your soul?
Indent your individuality so you can
now fit on the same page with them.
You were never trendy; I mean, look at your wardrobe.
But you needed something higher to reach for than the
American Dream.
It is always out of reach anyway.

And, besides, it feels good to think, with a little finesse, that
maybe, just maybe, this time it can work—we can all be one.
Without class distinction is a classy way to live.
Let's share the wealth, property, the coronavirus.
Welcome to the petri dish in the laboratory of the lemmings.
Come let us sip a latte with Lenin,
drink tea with Stalin from the samovar of Satan.

But first, let us carefully peruse the sanitized, revised manifesto *CliffsNotes* version of this experiment.

Ask, if you dare, why there's no mention of the millions of people, just like us, who once sat at a table feeding on the same collectivist utopian-flavored breadcrumbs and then found themselves picking out rat hairs from bowls of Gulag goulash.

Haiku-Dos

1.
Snail
Tired
Of the pace
Enjoys a ride
In an escargot-kart

2.
Earth
Seeking to be happy today
Though often stricken
With terra

3.
I'm
Out of sorts
Does anyone have
Any sorts?

4.
I was thinking of taking up Kung Fu
But I'd rather do
Kung Pao

5.
Being quasi-positive
I feel like I'm skating
On thin ice
But about to have
A breakthrough

6.
Can zombies get healthcare?
Or is death
Considered
A pre-existing condition

7.
I'm too qualified
To do
Anything

8.
Sometimes
The envelope
Pushes back

9.
At the supermarket:
Cashier: "Did you find everything you're looking for?"
Me: "Do we ever?"

10.
There's got to be
A better way for how
Not to make a living

11.
I'm a bit
out of touch
I thought Wikileaks
Was a bladder problem

8 PM

Driving to the gym,
I talk to God.

"I am sorry," I tell him.
"I love you, and I'm sorry. I fall so far short."

I stop in front of the Waffle House.
My tears are not salty, but sweet,
like the sacred syrup tapped from the Tree of Life.
Does forgiveness have a flavor?

I don't want to breathe.
Or move.
Or talk.
Or think.
Or do anything.

I just want to sit
parked in my Subaru
in the gym lot
forever.

And just be loved,
like this.
Oh God,
like this.

Why do these
five minutes of
unsolicited epiphany
have to end?

I check in at the gym desk and go
straight to the basketball court.
Shawn looks at me and says,
"You've just been with a woman.
Look at him, he's just been with a woman."

"I've just been with God," I reply.

He does not know what to say.
We play two games of Horse.
I win both games and leave.

I can't wait to get home
and be with my wife.

Responsibilities

I'm walking through a supermarket.
Its slogan is, "It's Your Store."

Who needs this pressure?
I don't want a store.

All I want is a half-pound of Swiss cheese and some grapes.
I can't even handle pulling weeds in my backyard.
Now I'm responsible for the livelihoods of
150 employees and their families?

I'm thinking:
What if the New Zealand lamb is freezer burnt?
Is it my fault?

What if the produce guy
has marital problems
and comes to work
and ices the fish guy?
Now I'm a character witness.
Around the clock interrogations.
What if I crack under the pressure
and confess to killing Hoffa?

It's not my store.
It's not my world.
It's not the way it all appears.
It's not going to end too soon.

I get my Swiss cheese and some Chilean grapes.
The grapes are saturated with talcum-like pesticide.
They look like purple-eyed cataracts on a string.

I'm now at the checkout line.
The cashier fails to ask
if I found everything I needed today.

It's my store.
I could have her fired for that.
But I'm not that kind of boss.

Mary Apocalypse

The theater is full again tonight.
"Chim Chim Cher-ee. Supercalifragilisticexpialidocious."
A great time is had by all.
We feel safe.
There is no danger here.
What more we could we ask for?
A musical that makes us feel good about ourselves.

Magical.

For two-and-a-half hours we feel "Practically Perfect" about the state of the world. A handful of people in rows G and H realize that soon the earth will explode like the ruptured appendix of a sumo wrestler overdosed on helium-flavored seaweed.

Perhaps a few in the mezzanine will concede that corpses on our city streets will soon "Feed the Birds," or that "The Perfect Nanny" will be gang-raped by hordes of lawless men with expired passports, probably in the fall of next year. It will be a time of Brimstone sans Treacle.

Some in the cheap balcony seats might admit that relatives in New Jersey could hand over their second cousins to death for just "A Spoonful of Sugar."

But enough of that. We are having a "Jolly Holiday." So "Let's Go Fly a Kite" and forbid the foreboding.

During intermission, Nancy, an usher in her late fifties, confides in me. She believes that Christ will soon descend from heaven with a shout and a trumpet and the faithful will be caught up with him in the air.

Ten minutes later, a woman with wired wings simulates flight across the sky with a song and a dance. This is not the Second Coming. *False signs and wonders,* I tell myself. I'm thinking, *Mary Poppins is a type of antichrist.*

I anticipate, before the evening is over, that Nancy the usher and I will be tortured for our faith. These are the last days.

And, as one of the final songs in the show warns us, "Anything Can Happen."

Yellow Submarine

In my dream, a yellow toy submarine ricochets off a wall and lands in a toddler's mouth.

I watch the sub sink down the child's throat like the USS *Grayback* World War II submarine with its eighty-member crew after being hit by a five-hundred-pound Japanese bomb from a Nakajima B5N bomber.

Yellow is the color of peace and happiness. But I'm panicked.

Butch Mingle from Chester, Pennsylvania was one of the crew members who died that day and never returned home to see his sweetheart Jenny Zucchi.

Jenny ended up marrying Gus Villanova, who worked thirty years in a soup plant labeling cans of minestrone and beef barley.

And the child can't breathe and I'm hyperventilating.

What was it like for Butch those last moments, crying out to Jesus and Jenny as his heart sank with the *Grayback*?

One time, on the midnight shift, Gus loaded the wrong labels on the conveyer belt labeling machine and the cream of chicken soup was pasted with a clam chowder face.

And now I'm turning the toddler upside down and banging on

its chest and back. Whose child is this anyway? It's not mine. What do I do? What do I do? We all live in a yellow submarine. What would Paul McCartney do?

Get me out of this dream, please. I don't want this child to die in my arms.

And what about Akiyama—his name means strong mountain— the pilot who sank the *Grayback*, joining Butch Mingle in the same sea of futility a year later, gasping for life with his last kamikaze's *sake* death breath.

Does this child have a name?

What if Butch Mingle had lived, had come home from the war, had married Jenny, had gone to law school, had raised three kids, and then died when an eighty-foot fast food sign fell on top of his truck?

What if Gus had married Joan Block, had opened an Italian deli, had played clarinet at weddings on weekends, and had made his own clam chowder?

What if Akiyama had never been born, never died?

What if Paul McCartney was with me to distract this choking child with his psychedelic song as I watch the toddler's face in my yellow submarine dream now turning blue.

Time Warp

Years pass and I think I will land safely.
But an unscheduled flight of memory
pilots me to that place I vowed never to visit again.

There I am with the same baggage,
unpacked years ago,
landing at the same gate,
greeted by Larry,
the same limo driver.

"Welcome back. Will you be staying long?"

"No, not this time," I tell him.

"That's what you said last time," he replies.

"I know," I say.

I excuse myself to use the airport restroom
and to book a return flight.

Last time I drove with Larry,
he took me
out
of
my
way

to avoid inconvenient road work
(he claimed).

I think I believed him then,
but not now.

Sometimes the devil is in the detours.

On Leaving

We leave things.
All the time, we leave things.
In the land of elsewhere. Somewhere.
Who knows where?
We leave cell phones and keys,
dreams and memories.

Some things take leave of us.
They don't miss us as much as we miss them.
They get tired of us: "Have you taken leave of your senses?"
"My senses? Oh, they moved back East six years ago."

And one day, I will take leave of this body.
Maybe at a table in a barbecue restaurant,
pieces of pulled brisket stuffed in my jowls,
face buried in a plate of fried okra.
I would regret not leaving the waitress a tip.

Maybe I'll fall down dead on a city street
on my way to the pharmacy.
Would people step over me on their way to lunch?
I hope someone might at least stop and lift my wallet.
I try to carry $20 in lunch money for such an occasion.

But I'm not worried; my body isn't who I am.
Before I hit the sidewalk,
I'll be walking the streets of the Heavenly Jerusalem.

Oh yeah, a literal city, literal streets of gold.
With a literal God, a literal Christ, literal angels.
And me, with a literal new body,
5'9", 159 pounds.
I thought about being 6'2",
but everybody expects more from tall people.

You ask me, "How do you know such things are true?"
I guess I left doubting a long time ago.

Is there a miniature golf course where I'm going?
I'd have to say I'm not sure.
On that issue, I have more questions than answers.
I always leave room for mystery.